NIGHT

OUT

Also by Vladimir Azarov

Dinner With Catherine the Great

Of Life and Other Small Sacrifices

Imitation

The Kiss from Mary Pickford: Cinematic Poems

Voices in Dialogue: Dramatic Poems

NIGHT OUT

Vladimir Azarov

Library and Archives Canada Cataloguing in Publication

Azarov, Vladimir 1935-
Night out / Vladimir Azarov.

Poems.
ISBN 978-1-55096-309-0

I. Title.

PS8601.Z37N54 2013 C811'.6 C2012-907914-6

Design and Composition by Hourglass Angels~mc
Typeset in Bodoni and Fairfield fonts at the Moons of Jupiter Studios
Van Gogh's painting "Undergrowth with Two Figures" (detail) is reprinted by permission of the Bridgeman Art Library International, New York.
Printed by Imprimerie Gauvin

Published by Exile Editions Ltd ~ www.ExileEditions.com
144483 Southgate Road 14 – GD, Holstein ON, N0G 2A0
Printed and Bound in Canada; Publication Copyright © Exile Editions, 2013

The publisher would like to acknowledge the financial support of the Canada Council for the Arts, the Government of Canada through the Canada Book Fund (CBF), the Ontario Arts Council, and the Ontario Media Development Corporation, for our publishing activities.

Conseil des Arts du Canada
Canada Council for the Arts
Canada
ONTARIO ARTS COUNCIL
CONSEIL DES ARTS DE L'ONTARIO
Ontario
Ontario Media Development Corporation

North American and International Distribution, and U.S. Sales:
Independent Publishers Group, 814 North Franklin Street,
Chicago IL 60610 www.ipgbook.com toll free: 1 800 888 4741

for Elza Ozol,

my lifelong friend

and talented architect

contents

II

VAN GOGH AND FRIENDS

III

KENZO TANGE

PREFACE

Night Out is my journey through memories – some imagined – a journey that begins with poems that focus on Russia, the country of my birth, and the ancestry of that great Russian poet, Alexander Pushkin: his great-grandfather was brought to Russia from Ethiopia by Peter the Great, and I have imagined an historical connection between Pushkin and the legendary Queen of Ethiopia, Sheba.

On such a journey, victimization must inevitably play its part. I have tried to capture that victimization by dealing with the martyr figure, Vincent van Gogh, by tracking him into the dark asylum of his sorrowful admiration for his friend, Paul Gauguin.

Finally, my background as an architect, and my recent trip to Japan, has led me to meditate on aspects of contemporary urban development, and so I conclude this book with a section of poems that touch on my favourite modern Japanese architect, Kenzo Tange.

V. A.

God tempers the wind to the shorn lamb.

–Laurence Sterne

Night Out With Peter and the Wolf

steel wheels clack
down the railroad track

clickety clack clickety clack

two tedious days of
a slowly clacking train
not like today –

this mail van   this mail car –
Germany to Moscow
Moscow to Berlin
The clink clink of a tin spoon
hot tea swirling in a thin glass –
German glass? yes – we Russians
still use thick glass tumblers for tea

my uncle Peter is the officer in charge here
Germany to Russia
– a railwayman –

clickety clack clickety clack
my guess is he drinks tea
and why not! that's how it usually is
among the passengers
always in the van
Ah-h-h! and could it be vodka
oh, such details – poured into the same thin German glasses

those days after WWII, the fifties
steel wheels down
the silver railroad track

clickety clack clickety clack

my uncle Peter who is in the German van
sipping his tea from a German glass
does not know that I know
Prokofiev wrote about tiny Peter and a Wolf
(from the local zoo)
something serious yet entertaining
tum tum ditty tum
as well as the text

this uncle of mine
who survived World War II
does not know who Prokofiev is –
he has a military job
totally appropriate

so I will tell him this childhood story
about Peter the Pioneer and a wild Wolf

I will tell my uncle Peter the story
after he takes me rowing
on the pond in Red Army Park
our oars dipping into the waves

plash plash plash

oh! it was pleasant idling in that rented boat
lying back watching the clouds drift by
and I was happy – but when we got back
to his family's small room – his wife
said to me – so strangely

"Vladimir – he never asks his own children to go for a row – "
I know why, I do,
though I say nothing to her
I had promised my uncle Peter
I would tell him this child's tale
about a Wolf from the zoo
and his boyhood days
when he wore a Hero-Pioneer's red tie

tum tum ditty tum

I will happily take a look at myself in the mirror
wearing the pale blue fake silk shirt
that my uncle brought me from Germany

my smile
and my uncle's wife's pout
(who is she to me
her name embroidered on our family?)
she moved the furniture around
preparing a place for the night –

I

PUSHKIN'S PATH

The Queen Partakes of Her Coffee: A Cantata

"If you do not know, most beautiful of women,
follow the tracks of the sheep
and graze your young goats
by the tents of the shepherds."
–Song of Solomon

what a time it was – goats
wreathed in bright berries!

bleating – oh, all of them cheerfully leaping!
a herder, Kaldi, and his flock are awake!

a smart goat herder swipes a fistful of berries
from a dancing goat

tastes, eats, chews, falls in love with the berries!
what is it? a laughing herder dances with joy!

a dervish on the mountain near Harar
dreaming of the fatted plains of Judah

the herder seems to be reborn – that's not him!
so who is he now? a new wise man! – Solomon?

Solomon with a bouquet of mind-bending berries
demands the Queen of Sheba not only come to him

but she must waltz on the mirrored floor –
so that she'll reveal her cloven hairy goat feet

(according to the Old Testament)
she dances passionately and after a few more sips

of an aromatic amber brew made from these berries
in a cornucopic silver goat's horn

the Queen spinning, leaping and – then –
oh – all the goats! oh – she has them whirling –

– so many dancing goats and she – O shameless Queen –
disrobing, half goat!

smart Kaldi – Solomon claims he's cut
a kid in two for the solemn dinner – but no! no!

the goat Queen cries! – babies embedded in the mountains
will dance between the razor-sharp stones – so

– Solomon sings his Song of Songs:

if thou know not
o thou fairest
among women
go thy way forth
by the footsteps
of the flock
and feed thy kids
beside
the shepherds' tents

the herder comes to his senses – he's come down
from the hills of Harar – he's about new business

forget Solomon, O Queen of Sheba!
join us at the Black Coffee House of the Ethiopian Kaldi –

our former herder – now the richest
merchant in Ethiopia, master of this dark berry

COFFEE! COFFEE! COFFEE!

Optimism, Why?

Fire up the bulbs!
The bulbs are all lit

So brilliant   so bright   they shine –
The sky so cleanly lit, so intense

The stars are cold and clear
The moon shy and naked

Showing her full face
Lit by all the fired-up bulbs

The sun? The sun doesn't object
And adds to the illumination

Calling the world's light to flare
Beaming its electric glow at her

She is the illumined and enlightened love
Of kings and princes who lack lustre

The light of all the sky-hung bulbs
Transforming blind atomic electricity

Into her beaming face
And you need her

So plainly and simply
You shine

So brightly and so purely
Because you command the bulbs!

So light up and purify the sky above!
Every light is shining now

Coffee Sipping

For some time each day's gone by un-
Accounted for, but now

I number every day –
New well-lit sunny days –

Long drawn-out mornings
Languorous noon hours –

Sip after savored sip soothes me
Adrift in dreams of Pushkin and Sheba

What happened? What's that?
Habitual lighthearted things disappeared

Morning breakfast is hit-and-run
Coffee sipping has become a gulp

Lunch, dinner, or supper,
Illusive joys pass speedily –

What happened? Nothing –
Nothing? Yes – naturally nothing –

Someone knocked at my door
Or opened it after not knocking

I set down my coffee so I could answer
The cup grew colder than winter in Russia

Pushkin ~ Three Translated Poems

ONE

I'd forgotten in my heart
How to weep, how to suffer pain,
How, through poetry, to impart,
In all its rapture, love. Never again,

No, I thought, love will not come again.
Amen.

But then – in the wine-dark sea
Of ecstasy, I revive,
Tormented, tearful, I thrive;
Words rhyme, come alive in me.

TWO

O beauty, do not sing a song
Of your sad Georgia to me:
In my old memory I long
For a far shore and distant sea.

You sing a song of strife,
Of steppes lit by moonlight;
And listening, I see a different life,
My missing love's unhappy plight.

The ghost in my blue dreams,
Though unreal, is with me more.
A phantom, beckoning, preens
In a sea breeze above the shore.

O beauty, do not sing a song
Of your sad Georgia to me.
And in my memory I long
For a far shore and distant sea.

THREE

Why call my name
When you know it will lie
As still as the sound of night
On a forest floor, or,
Will soon recede from sight
Like a spent wave on the shore,
Its only trace my unknown
Epitaph carved into the face
Of a weather-beaten stone?
Why call my name?
What comfort to you
Are memories of me –
Your emotions askew?
Souls perish, set apart.
Yet, you may, one day,
Amidst some new sorrow, say
You cherish me in your heart.

Scan the QR for Vladimir Azarov's recitation of the Pushkin Poems (a part of the book's video Trailer for *Night Out*).

Or view at: www.tinyurl.com/Azarov-NightOut-Trailer

II

VAN GOGH AND FRIENDS

Pointillista Sonata

swirls of white – helter-
skelter snowflakes

my backyard
point by counterpoint of colour –

a pale translucent winter
of painted snow

a total whiteness
a grey-haired landscape

trajectories of zigzagging flakes
the bare branches gently shaken

by light winds
cold dreams breathing

belonging to their mother – a birch stand
asleep in

ice-bound December soil
heated by an underground parking garage

my backyard – urban parkette birches
emigrants estranged

swirls of white
blending into the milk-white birch bark – portion of

a pointillist white canvas...
but I remember – yesterday was spring

below zero Celsius on the window's other side
where swirls of white devour my garden

Night Out With a Painter's Case

hey! kind Arlesians! hard-working folk!
don't mock this man who's only out for a walk

straw hat brimming his red hair,
backpacking a heavy painter's case

hey! peasants parting those high green grasses!
reaping sheaves of ripe wheat

lead him out of your high French fields where he's been painting
wavering gold images of the wind

hey! you women with your frilly white sun bonnets
who remind him of Breton maidens sprouting white wings in the rain

from those stones in the Rhone where you do your laundry
beckon to him with your sunflower hands

smile at him the way women smile at men!
not at his haggard asylum face, the one he drew in Saint Remy

don't tease him – hey! you nasty little bully boys!
don't threaten him with picket slats and stones!

Gauguin, his only Paris friend,
carries his sword out of the Yellow House

Vincent thanks you, Gauguin, for your perfect drawing classes but
please don't argue with him about his ideas

caw! o ravens! cry and flee from his sky
with your black, scarifying silhouettes!

don't torment him with those dark crooked shadows
that hover just beyond his sorrowful canvases

Starry Night

waltzes in a gyre
of endless cobalt emptiness

a darkness where the hands of God
course through the ardent abyss

cosmic brush strokes
tailing through yellow comets

attuned to taut strings
the echo of an unsleeping life

a settling land
enveloped in a dreamy stillness

a golden dance of sparks
lights the starry suns

the canvas is night's self-
portrait in an asylum

"Les Miserables"

no bucolic festival of dancing sylphs
lit by various heavenly rays;

no dissolving airy watercolour shades
on the oil canvases of both sexes' bodies

just hard-edged truth
a strict bald-faced style that forces

onlookers to turn to other more neighbourly walls,
to a sweeter, plainer beauty

the two painters were friends and outsiders
– Van Gogh and Paul Gauguin

"We are 'Les Miserables!'" said Gauguin
their works unsuccessful

in the Paris salons –
"Les Miserables" is the name of his

self-portrait – a reference to Victor Hugo's
hero Jean Val Jean

a convicted bandit, a criminal saint
'Miserable' in his life

"Les Miserables" we are!
"Why?" asked Van Gogh

"Why is it the public doesn't love us?
it's so simple" –

and he repeats "We are 'Les Miserables'"

The Yellow House

Through a window, as he ruffles his
Red hair, he stares at the newborn sky

Metallic hawk eyes reflect
An orange morning sun

Dawn of a reluctant smile
As he turns to his paint pots and easel

Intense, he sits and closes his eyes
Smells coffee's urgent aroma

Gauguin is in the kitchen cooking
Pungent thinners in the air irritate him

His canvas rattles on the easel
At an unexpected noise – a shot!

A spatter of squeezed yellow flies
Straight from tube to canvas!

A future painting sighs, serene:
Van Gogh begins to ramble

Joanna's Interview

I am Joanna, wife of Theo, brother
to Vincent Van Gogh

no, my husband did not ask me
to bury him close to his loving brother

at the great artist's final resting place
in Auvers-sur-Oise's new cemetery

against the stone wall under the tolling
of a church bell

oh, you are right, to maintain the honour of our children
we should lie shoulder-to-shoulder as real spouses

but tragic Vincent altered all tradition
God couldn't save him

his revolutionary passion in need of
a constant guide if only in his afterlife

no! no! foolish rumour!
I answer directly – I do not wear

the shame of a sham morality – I would
like to see him off to paradise

Vincent was obsessed by his own artistic madness
proximity is a blessed balance

for their souls, isn't it?
poor Vincent... used girls just as models

in conclusion I claim – a wife's finest
calling is to be a philosopher

Who Cut Off Van Gogh's Ear?

> *"... the truth is much more complex than the story*
> *we've all known."*
>
> –H. Kaufmann and R. Wildegans,
> *Van Gogh's Ear*

The artist sits in a dream on a gallery bench,
Brooding, resting, watching,
Conjuring a bouquet of cut sunflowers
A sunny field, the binding summer heat
Hands still not free enough
To set the bright yellow bucket in its ceramic base
To seize each colour and to brush
The canvas' face with coarse bristles
After rowing alone on the Rhone

Pale tense face portrayed
A blue, green and
Yellow palette
The twinkling eyes tightened
To hide their huge pain
Painted? Artificial?
Or by nature alive?

Is it a picture in a frame?
Frozen yet articulate
A still life live portrait of

A lone figure sitting on a gallery bench
Or in a boat now alone and rowing on the Rhone

Brushed gold or silver framing
Of a look
Hawkishly angry
Or persecuted under a broad-
Brimmed hat
And burnt red hair
Not like so many familiar faces
Capturing the gallery goer's
Expression – bland observation –
The faces look out from their frames
Frames of brushed silver or gold
A framed mirror
Reflecting the face of
A lone figure sitting on a gallery bench
Or alone in a boat rowing on the Rhone

A creased white cloth
Binding the painted face
As he sits on a bench
Touches the swollen bandaged wound
Rainbow rain over the Rhone
Yellow, green, blue, white
Spanning a canvas
Playing, shivering
In harmonic silence
Or, in the cacophony of

A lone figure sitting on a gallery bench
Or in a row boat on the Rhone

Yellow House Redux

The last sweet drop of absinthe
Stills his mind

As he stares at a silhouette
Or simply at the face

Across the table –
Scattered thoughts out of focus

He doesn't feel the closeness
Of his mercurial friend

Vincent Van Gogh hates Paul Gauguin
The arrogance of his smile

His haughty look
Blade nose of a Parisian snob

An unpleasant gaze
Emanates from Van Gogh

Hatred boils the artist's blood
A blaze of blinding light dissolves

All the colours of his life –
Red, green, blue, yellow

His animated saviors are on the run
Flying from him –

Like his aesthetic friendship
Soon his staring eyes are threatening:

"Hey, hey, traitor!
Begone to your lecherous Paris!"

An empty thin glass caroms off Gauguin's cheek
Van Gogh does not hear the ring of

Shattering glass on the ceramic floor –
He opens his eyes in the morning

Stretched out in his small wooden bed –
Gauguin is disappeared forever

Rachel

His whirling thought
after rowing on the Rhone –

fighting with Gauguin, his friend, off-balance
in the boat– not the best place to try a punch

then, after gingerly stepping to the top of the riverbank,
his heels clacking on cobblestones,

bandaged, he darts into a bordello –
to his only friend and model, the prostitute Rachel:

"Oh, Rachel hide it! hide it quick as you can!
This bundled package in my pocket –

I ask you, dear girl – hide it
in with your fancy lingerie –

intimate witness to two men
arguing all night in a boat –

No! no! – it's not my foreskin or Gauguin's!
Rachel! don't talk like that! Please

A lobe! it's only the lobe of an artist's ear –
the ear of Vincent Van Gogh!

Hide it, Rachel! keep quiet!
How come you're fainting?

A bloody bandage? It's for my self-portrait!
Thank God – an accident, no gunshot!"

She knows how hot tempered they are –
She's been with both of them –

Rachel quits her bed
and goes to the Arles police...

Is That a Picture in the Frame?

This pale, tense face
Blue, green, yellow –
Strange?
With the twinkle
Of something in hiding behind the eyes?
Is the face painted? *Ars* artificial?
Or natural? Alive?
Stilled? Frozen?
Living, moving, breathing?

Enough!
Stop yelling! Don't break our Pact of Silence!
On the river too! Do what you want!
Paris is your oyster!
Don't dissemble with me in the night! Sit still!
Don't rock the boat! Come to your senses! Stop shaking!
I can't keep my balance!
I'm falling out of the boat!
I'll fall down!
To the bottom of the Rhone!

Face face face –
One two three – three four five – five six seven –
There are so many faces!
The sad face, over and over,
The same look on the face, his face?
The face, as it stares, as it pleads, from inside the frame,
Becomes a mirror –
Is it his real face,
Anxiety-stricken, framed?

Give me the oar!
An oar! Give it to me! In my hand! No! No!
Not your dangerous hand! An oar!
What glistens in the dark? What shines
Sparkling sharply in the hand you hold out to me?
No no no – your hand!
Just give me an oar! Or I will get it myself!
I've got an oar! I will row!
I can defend myself with this wooden arm!

Framed
By gold or silver
Sad dismal wolfish
Look
The look hawkish
Or persecuted
Under a broad-brimmed straw hat
And red hair burnt

God! Devil! The pain! Sweat
Pours down my face
In my sticky blood I keep some measure of warmth!
Your cruel madness is not like mine! Sailed across many seas!
My ear and your oar are in
My hands! Away! Don't touch me! I row
To the river bank! To staunch the bleeding!
Toss me your handkerchief!

A dirty creased white
Cloth binds
The face where the whole
Canvas is

Composed of pain
Yellow, green, grey, white
Shivering
With the cacophony
That is, for me,
A harmony

After

After Van Gogh's plunge into
The trembling purple of Gauguin's occluding silence

After his own crying windy noisy whirl
Firing madly brushed colours into life

The torturous unfortunate
Bright sunflower-yellow

Green-blue cucumber-grass
His thick rude scary volumetric brushes

He pleads for mercy from the world
And a silence shuns him

"O! come unto me, friend Paul!
Come to my blood-drenched bed!

Don't go back to Paris!
Arles has our Yellow House!

Submissive, there'll be no mad scandals from me
Not a word to my brother Theo

Let's keep to our Pact of Silence...
Gauguin quit Arles the next day

And the two men never saw
Each other again

A Dream Letter

> *"Gauguin said to me this morning, when I asked him how he felt: 'That he could feel his old self coming back,' which gave me great pleasure."*
>
> –Van Gogh, *'Letter to Theo'*

I am happy I've got your letter
I hear you are well

I hear with the only ear I've got
Safe, unscarred

I hear the postman's step on the stairs
The clacking of his steel-clipped heels

The tearing open of an envelope
A rustle of paper

The scratch of an ink pen
The tense engine of your breathing

While writing this letter
Like the painting of a canvas

I hear all the sounds
One ear is enough

I hear because your letter is a dream
I hear because your letter was a dream

I won't open my eyes
To see my old papered wall

Sun-faded partly virgin
Where the canvas is larger than the frame

Painted as often as that straw chair
Empty now with no one at the table

With a wine glass or a tea cup
So many things empty on the table

Gaugin: Tahiti and the Sword

Razor, knife?
Nobody needs them any more

On the wall –
A fencing sword

Hangs at ease
Cherishing its cheerful play

The forgetful sword doesn't feel blood
Behind the steel mask –

Blood flooding in on itself
Has nothing to do with the thinking sword

Through the pale shivering
Of human vessels

Blood courses along
Its crooked channels

Overcoming all obstacles
It reaches its own Rhone

Blood dissolves
In the Rhone's body

So far from warm Tahiti
Still reaching out to touch it

Night Out With a Nightmare

is it a nightmare or
a real daytime night insane in my asylum

noisy rustle of prickly grass
metal clack of my heels on the run

a streak of open door
the naked prostitute Rachel

also a naked man who pushes me
as he runs away

my fingers' silky touch on the light wool blanket
and after – a foliating spot of blood

on a fallen package wrapped in paper
hiding my razored ear

no – it is my wooden bed – the one you've seen
me paint in yellow – I realize

I realize there's a sticky black-red around me –
a stain widening

down between the floor planking
and my ha ha! –

I laugh, smile holding
a mirror's handle made of goat's horn

Van Gogh: The Rhone's Coldness

The silver Rhone is cold
A damp chill – a fever

Under the broiling southern sun where
Even the sky sweats

Sun's beams like arrows
Burn

Pierce deeply and reflect
Off the phosphorescent water –

Within a flat-bottomed mirror
Bordered by two banks – green gold yellow

An insidious cross-hatching of lines
The blood runs cold –

Crows scoring the flaming sun
Traverse this world into the next

Fragments of storm clouds
Instant necessities with nowhere to go

Their chill luminescence
Is a shroud over an extinguished fire

Their wings spread against a lightning strike!
O my damn fever under the shining sun!

O big black birds! Lend me your dark cover!
All I ask is that you leave me alone

With my mind and feelings intact
I ask for a wise smile oh just once from God

Japonism

"It is as simple as breathing."
–Van Gogh on Japonism painting

you are now seen all over France
a fresh impression of the Impressionists
French painters on the edge –
Manet, Degas,
Toulouse-Lautrec, Gauguin!

the time is 1854
with the treaty of Kanagawa –
the American and Japanese
isolation of Japan ends –
O Japonism!

you are found by Van Gogh
in 1885 in Antwerpt
on woodblocks he bought

O Japonism! your
kimonos, fans, and antiquities
became his April in Paris

Claude Monet's wife wearing
a kimono becomes a painted geisha
holding a Japanese fan

Vincent Van Gogh – coming to France –
settles near the Montmartre
Bing Gallery – the Japanese arts collection!
so – he – wearing a kimono
and Japanese *getas* on his feet
imitates Hiroshige and Hokusai
and Shusho also –
an avid collector of *ukiyo-e*
he has collected so many woodblocks

O Japonism!
you are in Van Gogh's

Bridge in the Rain – Plum Tree
in Bloom – Van Gogh's transcription

of Japonism in Arles
where Van Gogh shaved his red head
to be a monk in a Shinto temple

the intense energy of "Japonism"
encroaches on his mental asylum –
a martyr shoots a bullet into
his head – the end of Japonism in Europe

III

KENZO TANGE

"Tradition can, to be sure, participate in a creation, but it can no longer be creative itself."

–Kenzo Tange

At the Tomb of Kenzo Tange

> *"Now you must repent and turn to God,*
> *so that your sins may be wiped out."*
> –Peter's Letter to the Romans

I am here
my first day in Japan
at the Cathedral of St. Lady Mary
by Kenzo Tange –

here under a concrete tent
the steep massive vaulting
stepping out of an urban morning
into the tonally grey vision of Kenzo Tange

I am here
under the two gigantic wings of
Kenzo Tange's
"metabolistic" concrete flight
isolated in form from all the world –

I am here –
inside life – or death –
at one with a great Cathedral –

the unmoved mover
torn by a glimpse of symmetry
toward light in its flight

a narrow window –
a vertical shining crucifix at
the epicenter of the altar –
God in His Heaven can see
Kenzo Tange's great interior

I hear mass with my sophisticated lady friend
Yuki is her name – Hisako in Japan – but for all of us –
her European friends –
she is Yuki
patient, steadfast in her focus on her studies –
Japan to Canada

Canada to England
England to Japan

we are here
among lively animated faces
the crowd at prayer in the pews
projected onto the grey roughcast
walls that resonate Golgotha

we are here and Yuki smiles
a ritual performance at the holy table –
a procession of white-robed priests –

in their spiritual step dance
sacred words elevate
accompanied by the blare of an organ
announcing the blessed embarkation
of the church's mammoth ship –

a ship not of fools – not of Noah
but Tange's genius
a sacred structured cruise

his structuralism
after Le Corbusier's, after all the Swiss-French
structures – and Kenzo is his disciple
a gospeller here in Tokyo spreading the Word

though we dream of flying
I confess I do not know
how heaven has spread its wings above us

as for the pull of my own gravity,
I do penance

Seven Laconics on Silence

> *"Never rely on the glory of the morning*
> *or the smile of your mother-in-law."*
>
> –Japanese proverb

1.

listen to silence
the bamboo and cherry tree
sound silent at night

2.

the shady blue night
ignites a fallen star spark
a broken glass clinks

3.

sunny sky stretched
with wide white cloud teeth smiling
rain is not yet gone

4.

water clear as glass
light penetrates the bottom
frog stares at a cloud

5.

the first heavy drops
tap tap dissolving in dusk
evening road steams

6.

wide oak's shadow gives
such a wide shade – white slim birch
feeling so jealous

7.

above rippling waves
neither bog's splash nor frog's croak
what was your lunch – frog?

Urban Night Out

weary-eyed
the city of Tokyo is seen
in a strobe staccato of lights –
trajectory
quick as sheet lightning or cosmic flight
the wild glass screens of a highway train
or sleek subway cars
reveal an endless looping embrace
of urban futuristic obstacles

observing all the tricks of overwhelming space
the 20,000,000 inhabitants
– it is not a joke –

see in the transparent sides of trains
all the sleight-of-hand built forms, of scales
of several types of
Euclidian and non-Euclidian
man-created structures

but within a severely confined building space
sculpted by the heroes of
Tokyo's deconstruction during the
latter 20th century

architects:
Kenzo Tange   Fumichiko Maki
Jun Mitsui   Kisko Kurokawa   and Toyo Ito!

see   the caprice
of these Metropolis gods

see   a Martian landscape
from a high suspension monorail!

narrow and small   the tiny
gaps between living cells
for these martyrs of Urbanism
the vertical crowded floors
stairs! stairs! stairs!
inside to outside up and down

curious
in my hotel's low bed
I open my eyes
who's shaking me?
who wakens me?

a pull-switch
swings   a pendulum gone wild
but the pendulum is only my ceiling lamp's pull chord

a pale sun elbows
its way between the backyard walls

a sudden earthquake
I am queasy   shaking
in my nightshirt and kimono
I dive into an elevator!

a young bell boy laughs
"sorry
this is the way our life is" –

o there's no way the geniuses of architecture and engineerin
will ever construct a futurist seesaw
to counter the swinging earth   yet
their urban skyscrapers
transform imbalance into
balance

King of Geometry

"Nobody untrained in geometry may enter my home."
–Plato

(*a first square*)

the geometric inquiring spiral
leads to a cosmic height in art beneath
the trembling restless ceiling of
being and time's reality

exploring and absorbing
all palpable
all objective
visual subjects
then this inquiry wanders afield
outside an obviously inscrutable existence
to solve the convoluted formulas
of abstract non-objective subjects

an epistemology that is
the comprehension

of life as art
as the geometric surgeon of inquiry's
poetic method
Kazimir Malevich

(*a second square*)

a Russian artist who plunges behind
being's mirror
to seize innovation
                                        in the laconic spirit
                                        of an iconic Slav
birth
                        of the main math micro molecule
or quark
of the two-dimensional
all lines and all surfaces
a many-coloured
SQUARE

a zero form graphics against words

a simple song
sonnet of living poetry
sounding much earlier than any philosophy
or prehistoric rock drawing but

the transcendental Square's presented by
                                        an artist on the coming
                                        revolutionary
storm's eve
                                        dangerous times for
humankind
given an inhuman
march
against the vulnerable images of ART

(*a third square*)

idealistic hope for an ideal future
a quick breaking up of all illusions
creativity's evolved into Dante's

dark inferno
where a new crux for the avant-garde is forgotten

a premature newborn dead at its
birth after a bloody Caesarean section
the post-coup's Red Rough Repression
of Kazimir Malevich

alien change
becomes accusatory material leading toward
conviction – Geometric Art
                as hostile anti-Soviet
propaganda
                on the heels of
                his successful Berlin exhibitions
        his lectures
for Bauhaus' Gropius
                his Klee Kandinsky's close confluence
his life with Futurism
                Cubism
                        Suprematism

(*the last square*)

however years went by and time's
spiral
Kazimir Malevich's trajectory
arcs ahead
to the incarnation
of future human dreams
the vibrant contour of the
Square
an artist's presence
in the world

Scan the QR for Vladimir Azarov's conceptual video "Black Square" which features *King of Geometry*, as read by Barry Callaghan.

Or view at: www.tinyurl.com/Azarov-BlackSquarePoem

Prayer of Prayers

"Profit and loss does not exist in the mountains
and streams, but in the hearts of men."
–Muso Kokushi (founder of Tenryuji)

the clacking of wood soles
is a solemn sound

the leaves of trees
and a grassy mound
announce an end to cherry blossoms
by April or early May
in the monastery garden

the clacking of praying monks in lock-step
their march at dusk
methodical   mechanical
day to day

but pay no attention to the passing of such sacred things
their souls fibrillating at the sight of
a man-made hill in the image of the Buddhist Mountain

the "Sea" of stone fragments
in the rock garden

holy sculpted stones and milestones –
"Lion" "Echo" "Green" – tree stones
the monks reaching their destination
kneeling on their ornamental rugs
on the plank platform outside
to take off their knocking shoes

the shrine at the temple of the Hogonin
their white toe socks nudge the spiritual purity that's within
the barely perceptible interior
a few candles light the moving and motionless silhouettes
the specious but unseen now densely decorated space

a local Japanese home in the Himalayan Heaven
dark-blue trembling shades out for a walk
orange gowns that transform to dark-brown

holy books and prayer wheels in the monks' hands
hardly visible   hanging
hieroglyphs

horizontal lines –
Tibetan ritual characters from religious scripts
o! – the bells ring – gongs gong
a start of the Zen
zza-a-a – zzum-u-u-m-m – zzen-n-n
zza-a-a – zzum-u-u-m-m – zzen-n-n
mmm-mmm-mmm-mmm-mmm-mmm
zzzz-zzzz-zzzz-zzz-zzz-zzzz-zzz-zzzz

the echo   resonance   reverberation
gong – gong – gong – gong – gong

it will be long – lon-ng lon-ng lon-ng

dzin-n-n-n – dzin-n-n-n – dzin-n-n-n
rin-n-n-n gg – rin-n-n-gg – rin-n-n-gg

zen – zen – zen – zen – zen – zen
it is zumming musically beautifully

life   love   birth   human   being   Zen –
then death   wars   illness   dragon   devil   hell
all all present in this scriptural shrine
all now part of the low hanging sky

so dense   so solid   so materially grey
so pregnant with rain
singing strings inside heaven's darkness

the monks' sing-sounding mouths
larynx   sinews   announce a
change in nature   a spring run-

off of streaming magic words
hovers in the complex structure of the temple's
wooden ceiling
then   arisen   they go higher and higher
through the tiled coloured dragoned roof

prayers sailing through clouds
above the snow-topped Himalayas

the temple candles gutter and go out
tired monks meditate not on their knees
but astride hard mattresses
in their intimate tatami-floored cells
a cautious rustle of night gowns

Six Monks

six monks seated
behind me
in mid-flight
from Japan
40,000 feet closer to the stars

six young Buddhist monks
in brash orange robes

six round naked skulls

sleep like babies now

one with an open after-work laptop
a second holds his book in hand
his eyes are closed
a third leans his head against
the shoulder of the second

their food is untouched
layered vegetarian sandwiches

sound asleep but their brains
unsleeping
atop Himalayan peaks
coasting at full speed
above the sinful earth

almost at Heaven's gate
the cosmos is a lotus blossom inside each
and a Japan they left behind
on their Buddhist business trip
withers on the branch as a petal falls

six unsleeping monks asleep:

as sacred trees spin in their skulls
as in a Kurosawa film they've never seen –
their divine world is poetry
their lives refined in bright imaginations
works of art one cannot imagine
behold them now...

ideographs on a blank paper screen
minds flowing along horizontal lines
of Tibetan plain characters

holy stones of the temple space
the virgin gravel fields
of Buddha's vision
the zig-zags of a garden's trim design

six monks hear the murmuring creek
the slight stirring of leaves in the trees
the angel voices of small dappled birds
a raven's cathartic cry

six monks are asleep
in lined formation
or chanting to a sunrise burning inside

they march beneath the Cloud Dragon
their orange robes swaying
tracking the wind   the young monks' brave walk
their *getas* clacking when they move as one

bells ringing and gongs sounding
to plunge again into the high-flying Buddha's sacred
concept
of life – flight – breath – death –

a world inaccessible for all the world
for all the laity
so far from heaven
and so much nearer than ever before

behind the eyes of sleeping monks
yesterday's spring evenings
emerald green cupolas of foliage
above the temple space
live in these huge curly April bouquets
of plum and cherry blossom
that are now past

the monks breathe the sacred divine air

the pink fragrant petals of tiny falling flowers
swirling like confetti or mortal tears
six sleeping monks
at home in their temple
at prayer wherever they go in the world

Swallows

the swallows' flight is swift
the flock's darting flash

appearing again at
the gate of a cloud –

this micro-drop cover
sailing slowly

its aerodynamics
of lightning in flight

even sunlight cannot spoil
as it plunges into sky cotton

melding among the clouds
turn, veer, lift, stretch

clench, tighten
shedding molecules

of water vapour
absorbing more but – see!

the sky is clear again
the sun is blinding

clouds have borne
the swallows to heaven

Basho's Journey

his father – a samurai of low rank –
wanted a military career for his son –
as was the way in Basho's day!

"but do not deviate too far from a notable's life! –
never work in the kitchen" – his father said:
"stick to what's traditional in our old family tree!"

at his father's funeral – a famous poet –
Matsuo Basho
made a sad speech: "apologies my father –

I liken my respect for you
to a samurai's sword on the wall
a semblance – your lustre – caught in the blade's sheen

I am a horseman on my way to Edo
to read, listen
to my new poetic *haikai no renga*!"

today's Edo (Tokyo) is neither too close nor too far
from the shrines and temples
of sacred Kyoto –

today you go by bullet train in two hours
when five hundred years ago an arrow
took more than five days –

Basho's horse is tired – a poet thought:
"join them and tell him a story – the horse is your
best friend on your long journey!"

and Basho told his haikus to the horse –
and the horse nodded in approval of
Basho's poetry

those three strict gasps
of cold raining air
were added to three cold water drops

dark rain, with no flashing lights around
Matsuo Basho leant an ear
to the damp cold ground, not to the clatter

made by the dangerous horseman – no,
to the deep
internal call of Mother Earth

"I hear your kind caring voice! Please sing
a lullaby that puts me to sleep
when it's raining – I need to get up early"

a smiling poet
lying at rest beside the babbling spring's
face, jumping frogs were happy!

oh! a famous guest from our chattering high society!
frog frog frog! – jump! jump! jump!
a few hours later the squinting sun's first rays

tried to tickle Basho's bare face ever so lightly
ashamed at waking a hardworking haiku poet:
the Sun said: "so sorry, Basho –

but it's time to take up your journey!"
birds twittering were in tune with the morning sun –
"Basho Basho Basho – hey! get up get up!"

and then all the choir: "don't be late!
the whole world awaits you in Edo
your haiku-haiku-haiku participles" –

Basho said – "thank you, birds, thank you, Nature!"
unrolling his latest scroll – "please, dear Sun – dry
up this script of mine – wet with rain

hey you! – you frisky butterflies and green grasshoppers
help me out – each and every droplet on my transparent
waterproof scroll is yours be careful – but

no nibbling at the characters – okay?

these characters are so important – it is my new style –
the trembling words are witness to my fascination
with those who are human in our land –

real nature and real land – a soil for the birth of all
the world, those inanimate stones
animated

I believe any god – Buddhist or Christian – frees me up
in my artistic life and allows me to escape my home
I unloosed the millstone around my patient neck"

Basho to the Sun: "Sun – why do you love me so much?
kissing me so generously?
why? just for my sunny poetry?

but I am not an angel – I am an ordinary man of
the Earth and oh I do not deserve
your gentling warmth, this easing of my loneliness"

Basho wrote to a friend:
disturbed by others,
I have no peace of mind

falling sick on the road
my dream has wandered off
into a field of dry grass

Why Is It Not Now

why is it not now
but long ago?

I run through wet grass
with the sunny morning
still moist – the dew on leaves
still not dry though
the noonday sun is in the clear sky

the horizon's horizontal line
drawn by a vertical embankment
is a magnet for freight trains
shunting
coupling and uncoupling

I sit on the grass and watch
the open unroofed cars – sienna-rusty-red –
sooted from the coal hills as if wearing hats
or strewn with splinters from stacked logs

the grass of the embankment
twinkling with crystal drops

I feel a tickling wetness
through my summer pants –
the soggy spongy soft carpet –
that will grow hard and prickly later
under the flaring sun
and my palms stroke the stringy stems

I want to lie on
the deep-green massive slant
which envelops all the space around –
this whirl of grassy lashes staring at the sun
overcome by many wise bright eyes –

they look up – very proud –
these small yellow flowers –
their glossy sticky centres surrounded
by tiny golden petals
oh – I remember them so clearly
but did not know and do not know now –
their unspoken names

Drowning

> *"When a man dies his lips*
> *smile a different smile."*
> –Anna Akhmatova, sonnet-elegy after
> Stevie Smith

he was drowning in an azure blue abyss –
memory of a rain-streaked childhood –
the crowd paled at death's abysmal kiss –
a leaden sky and Russian birch wood –

I remember him – the lively, larking boy
his mother weeping, her deaf moaning –
death snatched him – a bobbing toy
alas – not frantic but already drowning

sodden trees pursue life, its traces
I hear a sad boy's fear-struck cry –
"*why me*?!" – the answer in his grimace –
the blue of his abyss the azure of the sky

Oh I'm not crying out in the river of my childhood
but drowning – in a Russian birch wood

Acknowledgements

I would like to thank my wonderful editor Bruce Meyer.
I would also like to thank Barry Callaghan
for his editorial and cultural acumen.

I am also grateful to Michael Callaghan for his artistic contribution to this book, and to Nina Callaghan for her thoughtful advice with language in these poems.

Vladimir Azarov is an architect and poet,
formerly from Moscow, who lives in Toronto.
His books include *Dinner With Catherine the Great, Of Life and Other Small Sacrifices, Imitation, The Kiss from Mary Pickford: Cinematic Poems*, and *Voices in Dialogue: Dramatic Poems*.
Two new collections, *Territories* and *Monglian Études*, will be available in autumn 2013.